PART ONE

Significant Details

Major and Minor Details

Details affect your comprehension of what you read. This book has two goals. It aims to help you

- find the important details.
- see the purpose of details.

Details make up most of what you read. Some details are more important than others. The most important details contribute directly to the writer's purpose. They are essential to the point of the writing. These are called significant, or major, details. Those that are less important are minor details. Good writers don't include details that contribute nothing to the point. However, careless writers sometimes do. Details that are off the point are called irrelevant details.

Spotting Major Details

Major details are essential to the writer's point. Therefore, they are essential to comprehension. Here is a hint for increasing comprehension. As you read, ask yourself these questions:

- Which details are essential?
- Why are they essential?

In other words, ask which details are significant. Then ask what their significance is.

The Purposes of Details

Details are easy to recall when you know their purpose. That is the topic of Part Two of this book. Here are the main purposes of details, with brief explanations:

1. **to define** a topic or show what it is, as a dictionary defines a word
2. **to give examples** in an explanation, or to help a reader grasp a broad topic
3. **to describe** so that a reader can "see" the topic
4. **to give reasons** for an opinion or a fact
5. **to explain** a fact or idea
6. **to set a tone or mood,** usually in a story and sometimes in a biography
7. **to show character** directly or through the character's words, actions, or thoughts
8. **to advance the story,** either the plot in fiction or the true events in history or other nonfiction

You do not have to memorize these definitions. You do not have to memorize the types of details either. The important skills are these:

- telling the major details from the minor details
- deciding what the purpose of those details is

These skills require a good grasp of the skill of understanding the main idea. Are you sure that you can recognize and understand the main idea of a passage? If not, you should read *Understanding the Main Idea, Middle Level* before going on with this book.

Recognizing Significant Details

Preview Quiz 2

As a preview of what will be discussed in Part Two, try to answer this question:

What details would be used to tell what something is?

   a. details that give examples

   b. details that define

   c. details that describe

Begin reading Part Two to discover the correct answer.

Details That Define

Details that **define** a topic tell what it is. They are often part of the kind of explanation a dictionary would give. Here is an example of details that define:

A court is a body of government that administers justice and settles legal disputes. The word *court* also refers to a judge or to a courtroom. In most Western countries, including the United States and Canada, court decisions are based primarily on *precedents,* or earlier rulings in similar cases. Court systems in most European and Asian countries are based on civil law or the policies of the government. In the United States there are federal and state courts. The district court is the lowest federal court. The Supreme Court is the highest.

The first sentence states the main idea. The rest of the sentences state details that help define that idea. Not all of the details are equally significant. These are the major details:

> In most Western countries, including the United States and Canada, court decisions are based primarily on precedents, or earlier rulings in similar cases. Court systems in most European and Asian countries are based on civil law or the policies of government.

Sometimes you must decide which details are most important for your purposes. Suppose you wanted to find out about the court system in the United States. These details would be most important:

In the United States there are federal and state courts.

The district court is the lowest federal court.

The Supreme Court is the highest.

Details That Give Examples

These details are usually part of an explanation. They may help make a broad topic clear. In this passage, all the details give examples:

> Protective coloring helps an animal hide. Colors and patterns help the animal blend into the scene. Stripes on tigers make them hard to see in tall grasses. The leopard's spots hide it in the light and shade of low branches from which it drops onto its prey. The flounder changes color to match its background. The caribou goes from summer brown to winter white to blend in better with its setting.

For most purposes, two of the examples would be enough to remember. When studying this passage, try to recall two examples that you like most or that seem most vivid.

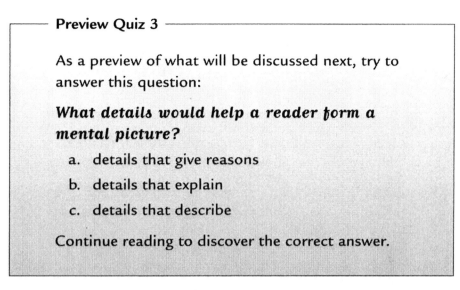

Preview Quiz 3

As a preview of what will be discussed next, try to answer this question:

What details would help a reader form a mental picture?

a. details that give reasons

b. details that explain

c. details that describe

Continue reading to discover the correct answer.

Details That Describe

Details that **describe** help a reader picture something. The details in this passage describe a setting:

> Farmhouses and barns were dotted about. They were the usual thing. Most were wood, painted white, with black shutters. Far up the sloping field to the right, though, were buildings of another sort. These were earth-colored. They seemed to be built of concrete, in a simple design. They were arranged in tiers, following the rise of the land.

In descriptions, the "big picture" may be more important than any one detail. Ask yourself what the point of the whole picture is. Then you may see that some details stand out. That is the case in this passage. In general, the scene seems to be a farming area. But something is out of place. The earth-colored buildings do not quite "fit" the rest of the scene. When one detail does not match the others, it is often the most significant.

Details That Give Reasons

Details that **give reasons** often support opinions. In the next passage, the last sentence states the opinion. The others state details to support it.

> The state senate wants to raise its pay 100%. These politicians are the best paid in the country! Is their work 100% better than it was? They are calling this raise an "emergency." That is outrageous. Even worse is their wanting the raise to be retroactive [having an effect on what is past]. Worst of all, future raises would be tied to state workers' raises. That means senators would get raises without a roll-call vote. Your NO vote at the polls will stop this outrageous increase.

The author tells the reader which details are major—from the author's point of view. Notice the words *even worse* and *worst of all*. These show the major details. The fact that the senators wanted the raise made retroactive is important. Retroactive raises would mean the senators would get extra money for past years of work. The author calls it "even worse" than other reasons. The author considers the point about future salary increases most important. It is tagged as "worst of all."

Suppose you were asked to write a response to the author's argument. You would be defending the pay raise. You would have to answer those points. They are the major details.

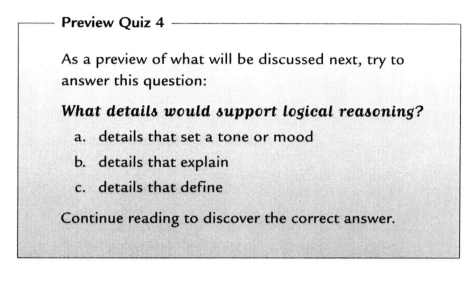

Details That Explain

Details that **explain** usually are part of logical reasoning. The reasoning is intended to make a fact or idea clear. Details help make facts clear. The passage below explains a fact about gravity. Notice how the details work.

> Newton's law of gravity tells us that the force lessens as the bodies move apart. Let's say that Star A and Star B are the same size. If they are the same distance from us, they both pull us with the same force.
>
> Now let's say there is a Star C. It is the same size as A and B. However, it is twice as far away. Newton's law says that its pull will be just one quarter of A's or B's.
>
> What about Star D, which is the same size but is half as far away? Its pull will be four times that of A or B. It will be sixteen times the pull of C.

Notice that the details can help you remember the main idea. Four examples of stars and their gravity are given. In one example, two stars are at the same distance and exert the same pull. In the second example, a star is farther away. It exerts less pull. In the third example, a star is closer. Its pull is greater.

In a well-written explanation, all the details count. You should be careful to think through the details. Try to restate them. Remember them with the idea they explain.

Details That Set a Tone or Mood

You will usually find details that **set a tone or mood** in fiction. Sometimes they appear in a biography. They may appear in other nonfiction that has a story to tell. Read the following passage from a biography.

> A terrible roaring noise woke me up, and I peeked out of the flap of my tent. Lightning flashed across the sky and a loud crash of thunder resounded in the woods. I trembled with fright as I peered into the night. Then came another deafening roar. I jumped back in terror. In the next flash of lightning, I saw an enormous bear ripping the food container. My heart pounded as I gasped for breath and uttered a faint cry. Panic engulfed me and I stood motionless.

Nearly every detail helps set the frightening mood. In this case, the mood matches the character's feelings. These details set the mood:

- trembled with fright
- jumped back in terror
- heart pounded
- gasped for breath
- panic engulfed me

When details set a mood, one detail often stands out. In this case, it is the last one—panic engulfed me. This is the major detail. It summarizes the feelings of the person.

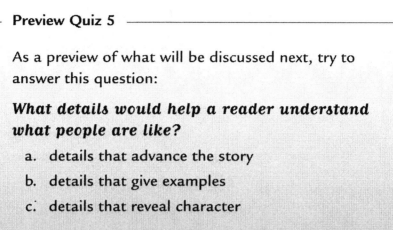

Preview Quiz 5

As a preview of what will be discussed next, try to answer this question:

What details would help a reader understand what people are like?

a. details that advance the story

b. details that give examples

c. details that reveal character

Continue reading to discover the correct answer.

Details That Reveal Character

Details that **reveal character** may do so in several ways. These are the most common:

- direct description
- the character's speech
- the character's actions
- the character's thoughts

Notice the character in the passage below. It is adapted from Charles Dickens's novel *David Copperfield*. In the passage David meets Miss Murdstone for the first time.

It was Miss Murdstone who was arrived. A gloomy-looking lady she was. She was dark, like her brother, whom she greatly resembled in face and voice. She had very heavy eyebrows, nearly meeting over her large nose. She brought with her two hard black boxes, with her initials on the lids in hard brass nails. When she paid the coachman she took her money out of a hard steel purse. She kept the purse in a very jail of a bag which hung upon her arm by a heavy chain. It shut up like a bite. I had never seen such a metallic lady as Miss Murdstone was.

Do you find Miss Murdstone unappealing? Does she seem threatening? If so, you have responded well to Dickens's description of her. So many details are *hard*. These include the boxes, the nails, her purse, and the heavy chain. She carries a jail-like bag. It shuts like a bite. The strong hint is that Miss Murdstone will be hard on David. She will treat him as a jailer would. This is just what happens in the book.

Details that reveal character usually add up to a general view. Look for the strong or unusual detail. It will be the most significant. In this case, it is the "jail of a bag" that shuts "like a bite."

Details That Advance a Story

Details that **advance a story** keep the story going. The story may be the plot of a work of fiction. It may be the events in a history or biography. Here is a passage from a short story. It is Stephen Crane's "The Open Boat."

> The men were silent. They turned their eyes from the shore to the comber [a long curling wave] and waited. The boat slid up the incline and leaped at the furious top. It bounced over it and swung down the long back of the wave. Some water had been shipped and the cook bailed it out.
>
> But the next wave crashed also. The tumbling, boiling flood of white water caught the boat and whirled it almost perpendicular. Water swarmed in from all sides.
>
> The little boat, drunken with this weight of water, reeled and snuggled deeper into the sea.

You can see that the boat is in trouble. The major details show the roughness of the sea. The detail most important to the plot is the very last sentence. It suggests that the boat is about to sink.

The sample exercise that follows will give you a chance to apply your understanding of details. Before you start it, reread the list on page 6 that describes the purposes of details. Keep them in mind as you read the sample passage.

PART THREE

Sample Exercise

The exercise on the next page is a sample exercise. It shows how you can put the information you have learned in Parts One and Two to use in reading.

The sample exercise also previews the twenty exercises that appear in Part Four. Reading the sample passage and answering the sample questions get you off to a good start.

The answers to all the questions are fully explained. Reasons are given showing why the correct answers are the best answers and where the wrong answers are faulty. The text also describes the thinking you might do as you work through the exercise correctly.

Complete the sample exercise carefully and thoughtfully. Do not go on to Part Four until you are certain that you understand the uses of details.

___ Sample Exercise _____

What makes popcorn pop seems to be a mystery. Actually, popcorn's great increase in size is no mystery at all. Each popcorn kernel has a hard outer covering. Inside each kernel is moisture. When the kernels are heated to 400° F (about 204° C), the moisture turns to steam. The hard covering bursts because of pressure. The result is a great treat.

The popcorn that we eat is much better than the kind our grandparents ate when they were very young. Scientists have improved it. In the 1890s a better kind of popcorn from Latin America was crossed with American popcorn. Later, Japanese hull-less popcorn was crossed with American popcorn. Today there are about 125 kinds of popcorn. Only a few of the best are planted.

Believe it or not, the popcorn plant is a grass. Popcorn itself is actually grass seed. Its proper name is *Zea mays everta.* So if you want to impress your friends, say, "Pass the *Zea mays everta,* please."

1. Most of the details in the first paragraph
   a. give examples of ways to enjoy popcorn.
   b. describe the flavor of popcorn.
   c. support the writer's opinions about popcorn.
   d. explain how popcorn pops.

2. American popcorn was improved by
   a. increasing the steam pressure.
   b. crossing it with other popcorns.
   c. shipping it to other countries.
   d. renaming it *Zea mays everta.*

3. The writer points out that
   a. popcorn is actually grass seed.
   b. scientists are searching for better kinds of popcorn.
   c. corn without a hull makes the best popcorn.
   d. popcorn is grown all over the United States.

4. Circle the paragraph in which details define popcorn.

Answers and Explanations

1. To choose the best ending, first read the choices. Then skim the paragraph. Decide what part the details play. You should see that the best answer is *d*. The writer explains how popcorn pops. The details are part of that explanation.

Answer *a* is wrong because there is no discussion of ways to enjoy popcorn. The details do not give examples.

Answer *b* is wrong because there is no description of the flavor of popcorn. The details do not describe.

Answer *c* is wrong because the writer states facts, not opinions. There are no opinions to support.

2. To complete this sentence, you have to find a significant detail. That detail explains how American popcorn was improved. First read the choices. Then skim the passage. Look for the key word in the sentence: *improved*. The best answer is *b*. American popcorn was improved by crossing it with other popcorns. This fact is stated in the second paragraph.

Answer *a* is wrong because nothing is said about increasing steam pressure.

Answer *c* is wrong because it doesn't make sense. Shipping popcorn to other countries would not improve it.

Answer *d* is also wrong because it doesn't make sense. Renaming popcorn would not improve it.

3. Again, you must find a significant detail. Read the choices. Skim the passage, looking for key words in the choices. You should find that the best answer is *a*. Popcorn is actually grass seed. The answer is found in the third paragraph.

Answers *b, c,* and *d* are wrong because they do not state details from the passage.

4. Skim each paragraph. Look for details that define. The last paragraph defines popcorn.

> Believe it or not, the popcorn plant is a grass. Popcorn itself is actually grass seed. Its proper name is *Zea mays everta*. So if you want to impress your friends, say, "Pass the *Zea mays everta*, please."

If you had any trouble answering these questions, review the passage and questions. If after that you still do not understand the answers and explanations, check with your teacher before going on.

PART FOUR

Practice Exercises

- The twenty practice exercises that follow will help you put to use your ability to understand details.

- Each exercise is just like the sample exercise you completed in Part Three.

- Read each passage well. Answer carefully and thoughtfully the four questions with it.

- Correct your answers using the Answer Key at the back of the book. Mark your scores on the chart on page 64 before going on to the next exercise.

Practice Exercise *1*

If you were searching for humankind's most dangerous enemy, you would not have to travel to far-off jungles. The animal you are looking for is the rat. Rats are big trouble in many ways. First, they are big eaters. A rat may eat one-third of its own weight in 24 hours. A person weighing 150 pounds (68 kilograms) who ate as heavily would need 50 pounds (23 kilograms) of groceries each day.

On farms, rats munch on corn, wheat, and other grains. They gobble vegetables and eggs. They kill baby chickens and pigs. City rats live in stores and homes. They run through the back streets at night, eating food where they can find it. Rats also destroy food by making it dirty.

The financial loss to rats in the United States alone is close to three billion dollars a year. The loss of human life because of rats can hardly be figured. Certainly millions of people have died from diseases spread by rats.

1. Most of the details in the second paragraph
   a. define a topic.
   b. give examples.
   c. describe.
   d. advance a story.

2. According to this selection,
   a. the most dangerous rats are found in jungles.
   b. rats look for food at night.
   c. fleas cause more disease than rats do.
   d. rats need very little water to survive.

3. The writer states that financial damage caused by rats
   a. is most common in cities.
   b. costs Americans billions of dollars a year.
   c. is on the rise around the world.
   d. cannot be figured in dollars and cents.

4. Underline a detail that explains how much a rat can eat.

— Practice Exercise **2** —

The first train passenger cars were simply stagecoaches mounted on four train wheels. When longer cars were needed, the old car design was dropped. Then the cars were made much like modern boxcars, but with windows in the sides. They were made with eight wheels—four at each end. They had hard wooden seats with straight backs. In winter they were heated by a small wood stove at either end. Light came from a few candles stuck in sconces nailed to the walls. Air in these cars was often smoky and unhealthy.

Changes in design came very slowly over the years. Springs were added to the wheels to smooth the ride. Vents were cut through the roof to draw out the smoke. By 1850 seats were made of soft leather. Candles were replaced by lamps. Not until 1872 did electric lights arrive, which provided better lighting in the cars.

1. Most of the details in the first paragraph
   a. describe.
   b. give reasons for an opinion.
   c. reveal character.
   d. advance a story.

2. In winter the early cars were heated by a
   a. gasoline burner at each end of the car.
   b. kerosene stove.
   c. wood stove at either end.
   d. coal furnace.

3. According to the passage, the cars were lighted by
   a. candles in sconces nailed to the walls.
   b. battery-powered electric lights.
   c. lanterns carried by some passengers.
   d. natural light alone.

4. Underline a sentence that shows how the ride was made smoother in later years.

Practice Exercise 3

The clothes the Puritans wore were picked for them, not by them. Church elders decided what clothes were "proper," and proper clothes were in quiet colors. Most clothes were black, but many were tan or brown or dull red. Collars, which the Puritans called neckcloths, and cuffs were white. At first the Puritans did not use buttons. The elders said buttons were vain, and being vain was being sinful. But by 1650 many Puritans, and the elders themselves, had begun to use buttons. The Puritan man wore a short sleeveless sweater called a jerkin. He also wore a doublet, which was a jerkin made with two layers of cloth. Some doublets had sleeves. Others had armholes with strings in them for tying on the sleeves. The strings were called points. The Puritan's pants, called breeches, were baggy and tied below the knees. Sometimes he wore splatterdashes. These were loose leggings that came up to his thigh and kept mud and water from splashing on his breeches.

1. Most of the details in this passage
   a. give reasons for an opinion.
   b. set a tone or mood.
   c. describe.
   d. advance a story.

2. This selection points out that
   a. the clothes of the Puritans were made of cotton.
   b. the Puritans liked bright colors.
   c. children wore the same styles as their parents.
   d. Puritans could not choose their own clothes.

3. The Puritan elders first felt that buttons
   a. were too costly for common use.
   b. should be used by women only.
   c. were a sign of vanity.
   d. had religious meaning.

4. Underline the names of three pieces of clothing used by the Puritans.

Practice Exercise 4

Two forces work to keep us from flying into space. The first is gravity, which pulls things to the ground. The second is a soft but thick wall called the troposphere (TROHP-uh-sfihr). That is the layer of atmosphere closest to the Earth—the air we breathe. At sea level, the air pressure (the "weight" of that soft layer) is about 14.7 pounds per square inch (101.3 kilopascals). It falls off quickly as you move above the Earth. Putting a spacecraft through the lower troposphere takes great thrust. So most rockets have sets, or stages, of engines. The first stage has enormous thrust to lift the rocket when it is dead weight. The second stage fires after the first burns low. The third stage fires after the second. It needs only a fraction of the thrust of the other stages. By the time it fires, the pull of gravity is less. The friction of the troposphere is also much less.

1. Most of the details in this passage
   a. define a topic.
   b. give examples.
   c. give reasons for an opinion.
   d. explain a fact or idea.

2. The passage says that the two obstacles to spaceflight are
   a. the troposphere and funding problems.
   b. the stratosphere and thrust.
   c. gravity and the troposphere.
   d. gravity and sets, or stages, of rockets.

3. The rocket stage that needs the least thrust is the
   a. first stage.
   b. second stage.
   c. third stage.
   d. tropospheric stage.

4. Underline the sentence that explains the purpose of the first stage.

┌─ Practice Exercise **5** ────────────────

Steam-powered cars were splendid automobiles. They were very fast. In fact, the first car to go 128 miles per hour (206 kph) was a Stanley steamer. It was in 1906, when cars were traveling an average of 15 miles per hour (24 kph). Some have estimated that the Stanley hit 197 miles per hour (317 kph) on a beach in Florida in the same year. This figure, however, is not considered official.

The steam car was loved by early owners for two main reasons. It was noiseless and it was easy to start. Doctors in cold climates liked the steam car because they did not have the time to handcrank a cold gasoline engine. The steamer could be left with the pilot light burning for quick, easy starts, even at two in the morning.

1. Most of the details in the second paragraph
  a. define a topic.
  b. describe.
  c. give reasons for an opinion.
  d. set a tone or mood.

2. A steam car traveled 128 miles per hour in
  a. 1886.
  b. 1900.
  c. 1906.
  d. 1919.

3. The steam car was loved by early owners because it was
  a. beautifully styled.
  b. cheap to buy and run.
  c. easy to start.
  d. very safe to drive.

4. Underline the brand name of the steam car mentioned in this passage.

Practice Exercise 6

I was born in the town of Lisbon, Maine, on a farm that my grandfather cleared from the wilderness. Life on a small farm in Maine then was very different from life today. This period was a time of hardship. The boom times were over. Still we had enough to eat, for we raised nearly everything we needed. We raised a lot of grain and always had ten bushels of corn and oats and five bushels of rye ground every fall. We had brown bread, johnnycakes, and Indian pudding. We had many other things I would like to taste just once more. We killed a big hog every fall and smoked the meat so it would keep. The rest we made into bacon. We ranged the country fields for berries to can for the winter, and often we had two hundred jars on the shelves in the cellar to carry us through the cold months.

1. Most of the details in this passage
   a. describe life on a farm in Maine.
   b. explain farming methods of the past.
   c. reveal the writer's character.
   d. advance a story.

2. Every fall the writer's family
   a. made maple syrup.
   b. went to the fair in Portland.
   c. cut wood for the long winter.
   d. killed a hog and stored the meat.

3. The writer spent much time in the country fields
   a. flying kites.
   b. looking for berries.
   c. playing games.
   d. baling hay.

4. Underline a sentence that shows how the writer's family prepared for the winter.

Practice Exercise 7

When George Washington became the first president of the United States in 1789, he had no idea that the country would grow so quickly. There were only thirteen states. These states were part of a narrow strip, about 1,000 miles long (about 1,600 kilometers), on the eastern coast. A census (population count) taken in 1790 showed that less than four million people lived in that area. The total population was only one-third the population of New York City today.

In 1781, Vermont was admitted to the new Union. It became the 14th state. By 1912 the country had 48 states. The 49th and 50th states, Alaska and Hawaii, were added to the Union in 1959. In later years people talked about Puerto Rico's becoming the 51st state. That idea, however, did not gain enough support to make it fact. Thus, it appears that the United States will consist of 50 states into the near future.

1. Most of the details in this passage
   a. define a topic.
   b. describe.
   c. set a tone or mood.
   d. advance a story.

2. The 14th state admitted to the Union was
   a. Alabama.
   b. Maine.
   c. New York.
   d. Vermont.

3. Alaska and Hawaii were admitted to the Union in
   a. 1934.
   b. 1847.
   c. 1959.
   d. 1965.

4. Underline the name of the place that people have mentioned as a possible 51st state.

Practice Exercise *8*

Leo Durocher, the great baseball player and manager, once said that Dusty Rhodes was the craziest-looking ballplayer he had ever seen. He wore his cap at a cockeyed angle. He ran with the speed of a tired blacksmith. His fielding was very uncertain. For a throwing arm, he might as well have been using a rubber band. But Durocher knew that Rhodes could hit. Because he could hit, the New York Giants, managed by Durocher, won the National League pennant in 1954. At the two most critical points of the season, it was Rhodes who led the Giants to victory. Playing mostly as a pinch hitter and a reserve outfielder, Rhodes went to bat only 164 times during the regular season. He hit 15 home runs and drove in 50 runs while earning a batting average of .341.

1. Most of the details in this passage
   a. define a topic.
   b. explain a fact or idea.
   c. set a tone or mood.
   d. reveal character.

2. Leo Durocher said that Dusty Rhodes ran with the speed of
   a. a crippled snail.
   b. a tired blacksmith.
   c. a bolt of lightning.
   d. an express train.

3. Durocher recognized Rhodes's ability to
   a. hit a ball.
   b. steal bases.
   c. field the ball.
   d. throw a ball.

4. Underline a sentence that tells what positions Rhodes played in 1954.

Practice Exercise *9*

Handball is a game played on a court that has either one wall or four. It was created by the Irish and was introduced into the United States by a man named Philip Casey. Like nearly all other sports, handball develops speed, strength, and accuracy. There may be two players in a game, one on each side, or four, two on each side. The first player or team to score 21 points wins the game. There were four walls in the handball courts until 1900, and a hard ball was used. About 1914, one-wall courts became popular because the game was played on the bathing beaches of New York. The game then spread throughout the country and became quite popular.

1. Most of the details in this passage
   a. define handball.
   b. give examples of games.
   c. give reasons for handball's popularity.
   d. explain how to win at handball.

2. Until the year 1900
   a. handball courts were made of clay.
   b. there were no rules for the game.
   c. handball was played outdoors.
   d. handball courts had four walls.

3. One-wall courts became popular because people
   a. began to play the game on beaches.
   b. wanted a simpler way to play the game.
   c. wanted the game to be more like tennis.
   d. liked to play the game on city streets.

4. Underline the sentence that tells who originated the game of handball.

— Practice Exercise *1 0* —

Meteor Crater in Arizona is sometimes called one of the great wonders of the world. If the Washington Monument were on the floor of the crater, it would not reach to the top. Today age-dating tests show that the meteor that formed the crater struck the Earth about 50,000 years ago. That was a time when huge glaciers still covered the northern half of North America. The meteor traveled toward the Earth at 30,000 miles per hour (about 48,000 kph) and struck the Earth with a force equal to that of a large hydrogen bomb. It killed plants and animals within a hundred miles. The crater was first investigated by scientists in 1891. For many years it was thought to be a dead volcano. In 1903 a man named Barringer bought the crater. In 1929 he proved that it was a meteor crater much like those found on the moon.

1. Most of the details in this passage
   a. define Meteor Crater.
   b. give examples of craters.
   c. give reasons for the opinion that the crater should not be
      privately owned.
   d. set a tone or mood.

2. When Meteor Crater was formed,
   a. dinosaurs roamed the Earth.
   b. ice covered the northern half of North America.
   c. volcanoes were active in the Southwest.
   d. the Earth was in the process of cooling down.

3. For many years people thought that Meteor Crater was
   a. an ancient burial ground.
   b. a place of early religious worship.
   c. a dried-up lake.
   d. a dead volcano.

4. Underline the sentence that tells the speed at which the meteor
   traveled through space.

Practice Exercise *11*

The lightning displays put on by thunderstorms can be more exciting than fireworks on the Fourth of July. The ancient Greeks thought that lightning bolts were thrown by the god Zeus to show his anger. They offered him wine and food in hopes that he would keep lightning from hurting them. The Norse believed that the god Thor caused lightning when he threw his hammer to the earth. This made sparks when the iron hit stones on the ground. Some Native Americans thought that the god of thunder was a great bird called the thunderbird. They believed that lightning was a flash of the thunderbird's eye. In the Middle Ages, people imagined that lightning was the work of witches. Many people carried splinters from a lightning-struck tree to ward off the dangers of lightning. Often church bells were rung to keep the lightning away. Ironically, many bell ringers were killed at their ropes when lightning struck the bell towers.

1. Most of the details in this passage
   a. give examples of beliefs about lightning.
   b. describe lightning displays.
   c. give reasons for fearing lightning.
   d. explain how lightning is created.

2. To please Zeus, the Greeks offered him
   a. valuable treasures.
   b. food and wine.
   c. choice fruit from their orchards.
   d. a freshly killed lamb.

3. The Norse thought that lightning was caused by
   a. sparks from a hammer.
   b. clashing swords.
   c. an angry star.
   d. gods in battle.

4. Underline the sentence that tells what group of people thought that the god of thunder was a great bird.

Practice Exercise *12*

The years 1880–1899 were called the Bicycle Age. During that time there were more than three hundred bicycle factories in North America. They made more than a million bicycles a year.

Today, there are more than 70 million bikes in North America. That is more than two bikes for every three cars. Within the last few years, orders for bikes have been so great that many factories are running three shifts of workers. They are still not able to keep up with the demand.

One factory boss said that people are interested in bikes now because of new interest in physical fitness. Another factory owner said that the problem of pollution helps sell bicycles. Certainly no one can deny that bicycles are inexpensive to use.

1. Most of the details in the third paragraph
  a. define the bicycle.
  b. give examples of kinds of bicycles.
  c. describe a typical rider.
  d. give reasons for the bicycle's popularity now.

2. During the Bicycle Age, bicycles were produced
  at the rate of
  a. one thousand a year.
  b. ten thousand a year.
  c. one hundred thousand a year.
  d. one million a year.

3. According to manufacturers, bicycles are selling fast partly
  because they
  a. are less expensive today than they used to be.
  b. are safer than motorcycles.
  c. do not pollute the environment.
  d. may be used by people of all ages.

4. Underline the sentence that tells how many bicycles are used in
  North America today.

— Practice Exercise *13* —

On February 12, 1809, Abraham Lincoln was born in a log cabin at Sinking Spring Farm near Hodgenville, Kentucky. When Abe was two years old, his father, Thomas Lincoln, moved the family to a farm at Knob Creek, ten miles (sixteen kilometers) north of the birthplace. In the fall of 1815, Lincoln and his sister Sarah were sent for a short time to a school a few miles from the Knob Creek home. In 1816, the Lincoln family moved once again, this time to Gentryville, Indiana. Lincoln worked on a farm where he split logs for fence rails and plowed fields. Later he was hired to run a ferry across the Ohio River. In 1828, Lincoln helped take a boatload of produce to New Orleans. On a second trip in 1831, Lincoln viewed the slave market there. His feelings against slavery are said to have developed during this trip.

1. In this selection the writer mentions
   a. the work of Lincoln's father.
   b. Lincoln's love for the wilderness.
   c. several people Lincoln knew in Hodgenville.
   d. some of the jobs Lincoln held.

2. Lincoln developed feelings against slavery when he
   a. took a trip to New Orleans.
   b. met a slave owner in Illinois.
   c. saw a slave being beaten on a neighbor's farm.
   d. helped a slave escape from a plantation.

3. Most of the details in this passage
   a. describe Sinking Spring Farm.
   b. give reasons for Lincoln's feelings about slavery.
   c. set a tone or mood.
   d. help tell the story of Lincoln's early years.

4. Underline the sentence that tells what Lincoln did when he worked on a farm in Gentryville, Indiana.

— Practice Exercise *14* —

An early ancestor of the horse lived in North America about three million years ago. Herds wandered throughout North and South America. Then for unknown reasons they disappeared. They left only skeletons for us to think about. The first North American horses of modern times were brought from Europe. In fact, Columbus brought a few horses with him on his second voyage to the Americas. He left the horses in the West Indies. In the 1500s the Spanish brought horses to North America. So by the time the English colonists arrived in Virginia in 1607, horses roamed the country. These horses were of no help to the colonists because they enjoyed their open plains hundreds of miles from the coastline of Virginia. It would be many years before these horses would be tamed by the early settlers who moved to the western plains.

1. Most of the details in this passage
   a. define the topic "horse."
   b. give examples of kinds of horses.
   c. describe a typical horse.
   d. help tell the story of horses in North America.

2. The first North American horses of modern times
   a. traveled in herds from South America.
   b. moved across the Bering Straits from Asia.
   c. were brought from Europe.
   d. evolved from early ancestors.

3. Experts are not sure why
   a. the colonists wanted horses.
   b. horses like to live in herds.
   c. the early ancestor of the horse disappeared.
   d. wild horses are difficult to train.

4. Underline the sentence that tells what European explorer first brought horses to the Americas.

Practice Exercise 15

For centuries, people have been celebrating the start of spring with fairs, parties, jokes, and good times. When the earth suddenly turns green after a long winter, people all over the world have felt the urge to dance, sing, and play jokes on one another. April Fools' Day goes back more than four hundred years to the time when the New Year's celebration fell on March 21 and ended April 1. Then people gave presents to each other on April 1.

In 1564, the French king adopted the calendar that we use today. Under the new calendar, New Year's Day was moved to January 1, but old customs were hard to change. Some French people kept giving presents on April 1. These people were called April fools. Gradually, people began giving silly presents on purpose and then saying "April fool" when the joke was discovered.

1. April Fools' Day can be traced back
   a. two hundred years.
   b. four hundred years.
   c. six hundred years.
   d. eight hundred years.

2. At one time the New Year's celebration began on
   a. December 1.
   b. January 30.
   c. March 21.
   d. April 1.

3. Most of the details in this passage
   a. give examples of April Fools' Day tricks.
   b. describe France in the 1500s.
   c. explain how April Fools' Day began.
   d. reveal the character of the king of France.

4. Underline the proof given for the statement "old customs were hard to change."

Practice Exercise *16*

Have you ever wondered where the story of Dracula came from? Wonder no more. Dracula was the creation of British author Bram Stoker. He wrote *Dracula* in 1897. It has been popular ever since.

The story of Dracula begins in Transylvania, a region of Romania. A lawyer from England travels there to get the signature of Count Dracula, who has bought a castle in England. As a guest in the count's mansion, he soon finds out that Dracula is a vampire and that he himself is a prisoner. He also learns that the count plans to take over England and change all the English women into vampires. The lawyer escapes and returns to England. He tells a doctor of Dracula's plan. Together they search for the evil creature and destroy him by driving a stake through his heart. With him die all the other vampires and the plans to conquer England.

1. The passage states that Bram Stoker's novel
   a. frightened many people when it was first published.
   b. was banned in London in 1897.
   c. was produced as a play in the 1920s.
   d. has been popular since 1897.

2. One of the main characters in *Dracula* is a
   a. young society girl.
   b. mad scientist.
   c. lawyer.
   d. police inspector.

3. Most of the details in the second paragraph
   a. explain what a vampire is.
   b. set a tone or mood.
   c. reveal Dracula's character.
   d. advance a summary of the story.

4. Underline the sentence that tells what the count's plan for England was.

— Practice Exercise 17 —

It is not difficult to make a vegetable garden. And the rewards are great. A few facts help in the planning stages. Before you plant, fertilize the garden soil by adding composted leaves, wood chips, grass clippings, sawdust, and vegetable garbage. All vegetables like sunshine—a minimum of five to six hours a day. So it is best to plant in east to west rows to get the most benefit from the sun. Tall plants such as pole beans and tomatoes should go in the rows at the north end of the garden. The low plants can go in the rows at the south end of the garden.

The three most popular vegetables to grow are beans, tomatoes, and peppers. Pole beans use little space and are ideal against a sunny wall or fence. Tomatoes should not be planted before the soil is warm. After the plants take root, tomatoes need little care. Peppers do well when they are planted near tomatoes. Peppers also need little care, yet they produce a good harvest.

1. Most of the details in the first paragraph
   a. define garden.
   b. give examples of vegetables to grow.
   c. describe various gardens.
   d. explain how to lay out a garden.

2. Most of the details in the second paragraph
   a. define garden.
   b. give examples of vegetables to grow.
   c. describe various gardens.
   d. explain how to lay out a garden.

3. Low plants should be planted at the
   a. north end of the garden.
   b. east end of the garden.
   c. west end of the garden.
   d. south end of the garden.

4. Underline a sentence that suggests types of fertilizer to use on a garden.

── Practice Exercise *18* ──────────

The house in which Abraham Lincoln died is located on 10th Street in Washington, D.C. It was built by William Petersen, a tailor from Sweden, in 1849. It is a three-story building. Since the house had more rooms than the family needed, extra rooms were rented to lodgers. The bedroom to which Lincoln was carried after he was shot was being rented by William T. Clark, a former soldier.

The Petersen house remained in the hands of the Petersen family until November 25, 1878. At that time, the heirs of William Petersen sold the house to Louis Schade for $4,500. Schade bought the Petersen house for a home and for an office for his newspaper.

Although the building was not marked on the outside, the Schade family was bothered constantly by tourists. They wanted to see the death room. Finally, in 1896, the United States government bought the building from the Schade family. Today the house is open to the public as a museum.

1. William Petersen worked as a
   a. soldier.
   b. tailor.
   c. carpenter.
   d. writer.

2. The extra rooms in Mr. Petersen's new home were
   a. used to publish a newspaper.
   b. reserved for government officials.
   c. turned into a print shop.
   d. rented to lodgers.

3. During the time the Schade family lived in the house, they
   a. were bothered by tourists.
   b. became wealthy.
   c. opened their home to the public.
   d. restored the home to its former design.

4. Underline the sentence that gives the purchase price of the Petersen home in the late 1870s.

— Practice Exercise *19* —

Scientists who study the life of ancient peoples have found much proof that people began traveling from place to place in very early times. Salt played a great part in setting up some ancient trade routes. It was not usually found inland, and people everywhere craved it. Therefore, it had a great trade value. Herodotus, the first Greek historian, wrote about a very old caravan route to the salt oasis of the Libyan desert in Africa. All through the ancient Near East, salt was a very important item of trade. It was carried along many early paths from one people to another.

One of the oldest Roman roads, the Via Salaria, or "Salt Way," was first made because of people's desire for salt. It reached from Rome to the salt beds of Ostia on the coast of Italy. Along it was carried salt for the "salary." When a Roman soldier was sent to a foreign land, he was given an extra amount of money to buy salt. *Salary* comes from the word *sal,* which means "salt."

1. Most of the details in this passage
a. define *salary.*
b. give examples of uses of salt.
c. describe everyday life in ancient times.
d. explain the role of salt in ancient trade.

2. The Via Salaria is the name of
a. an oasis in the desert.
b. a town in Libya.
c. an ancient road.
d. a seaport near Ostia.

3. In ancient times salt was so valuable that it was used
a. to pay Roman soldiers.
b. in expensive medicines.
c. in religious ceremonies.
d. to pay for expeditions to Asia.

4. Underline a sentence that tells that salt was found mostly in coastal areas.

Practice Exercise 20

In 1967 the United States Fish and Wildlife Service
listed alligators as an endangered species. Alligators were
killed faster than they could breed. Why were so many
alligators killed? Poachers, trappers who kill animals illegally,
were able to get prices that made it worthwhile for them to
kill the animals for their skins. Usually, the poachers
smuggled the skins in special trucks or in planes across
borders. This was often done under the cover of darkness in
areas where game officials were not likely to be posted. In
1977 the alligator population finally increased. Alligators are
now listed as threatened and not endangered. Today only a
limited number of alligators can be hunted.

1. Most of the details in this passage
   a. define *poacher.*
   b. give examples of goods made from alligator skin.
   c. describe the life of the alligator.
   d. explain why alligators became endangered.

2. Alligator skins sold for
   a. enough to make poachers hunt them.
   b. more than eight hundred dollars.
   c. more in some states than others.
   d. lower prices than crocodile hides.

3. *Poacher* is defined in the passage as
   a. the best grade of alligator skin.
   b. a type of gun used to stun alligators.
   c. a police official who protects alligators.
   d. a person who kills animals illegally.

4. Underline the sentence that states how many alligators can be
   hunted today.

PART FIVE

Writing Activities

The writing activities that follow will help you understand significant details. The activities will also help you use significant details in your own writing.

Complete each activity carefully. Your teacher may ask you to work alone or may prefer to have you work with other students. In many cases, you will be asked to write your answers on separate paper. Your teacher may ask you to write those answers in a notebook or journal. Then all your writing activities will be in the same place.

The activities gradually increase in difficulty. Therefore, you should review each completed activity before you begin a new one. Reread the lesson in Parts One and Two (pages 5–14) if you have any questions about significant details.

Writing Activity 1

Read the following passage from "The Storm" by
Kate Chopin.

Calixta, at home, felt no uneasiness for their safety. She sat
at a side window sewing furiously on a sewing machine. She
was greatly occupied and did not notice the approaching
storm. But she felt very warm and often stopped to mop
her face on which the perspiration gathered in beads. She
unfastened her white sacque at her throat. It began to
grow dark, and suddenly realizing the situation she got up
hurriedly and went about closing windows and doors.

Out on the small front gallery she had hung Bobinôt's
Sunday clothes to dry and she hastened out to gather them
before the rain fell. As she stepped outside, Alcée Laballière
rode in at the gate. She had not seen him very often since
her marriage, and never alone. She stood there with
Bobinôt's coat in her hands, and the big rain drops began
to fall. Alcée rode his horse under the shelter of a side
projection where the chickens had huddled and there were
plows and a harrow piled up in the corner.

"May I come and wait in your gallery till the storm is
over, Calixta?" he asked.

On a separate piece of paper or in your writing notebook, answer each of the following questions. If you are unfamiliar with any of the words in the passage, look them up in a dictionary or discuss them with your teacher before you begin writing. Your teacher may want you to share your answers with the class.

1. List details the author uses to tell that a storm is approaching. What does Calixta rush to do? What else does Calixta do in preparation for the storm?

2. In the first paragraph Calixta stops to mop her face. What does that detail tell you? Why would she need to do this?

3. Where does Calixta live—in an urban or a rural area? What details in the passage tell you where Calixta lives?

4. Why does Alcée Laballière come to Calixta's home? What details support your conclusions about why he stops there?

5. The details in the passage work together to create a mood or overall feeling. What mood do they create? How does the passage make you feel?

Writing Activity 2

Read the following passage from *Adventures of Huckleberry Finn* by Mark Twain.

The sun was up so high when I waked, that I judged it was after eight o'clock. I laid there in the grass and the cool shade, thinking about things and feeling rested and rather comfortable and satisfied. I could see the sun out at one or two holes, but mostly it was big trees all about, and gloomy in there amongst them. There was freckled places on the ground where the light sifted down through the leaves, and the freckled places swapped about a little, showing there was a little breeze up there. A couple of squirrels set on a limb and jabbered at me very friendly.

A. On a separate piece of paper or in your writing notebook, answer each of the following questions. If you are unfamiliar with any of the words in the passage, look them up in a dictionary or discuss them with your teacher before you begin writing. Your teacher may want you to share your answers with the class.

1. What do you learn about the setting of the story from the details in the passage? Which details about the place are more important? Which details are less important? Why?

2. Think about the squirrels on the limb of a tree. Is it an important detail? Explain your answer. How do their actions affect the mood, or overall feeling, of the passage?

3. Why does very little sunlight shine down on the young man? What details provide information that helps you answer the question?

4. How does the young man know that there is a breeze?

B. Look around your classroom. On a separate piece of paper or in your writing notebook, list details about the room. Does anything look out of place? What is hanging on the walls? Is there something that really stands out? Are there any notes on the blackboard? Are there any empty desks? What do the details tell you about the classroom? What overall picture do the details give you? Write a brief paragraph describing something about the room.

Writing Activity 3

Read the following passage from "A White Heron" by Sarah
Orne Jewett.

Half a mile from home, at the farther edge of the woods,
where the land was highest, a great pine-tree stood, the last
of its generation. Whether it was left for a boundary mark,
or for what reason, no one could say. The woodchoppers
who had felled its mates were dead and gone long ago. A
whole forest of sturdy trees, pines and oaks and maples, had
grown again. But the stately head of this old pine towered
above them all and made a landmark for sea and shore miles
and miles away. Sylvia knew it well. She had always believed
that whoever climbed to the top of it could see the ocean.
The little girl had often laid her hand on the great rough
trunk and looked up wistfully at those dark boughs that the
wind always stirred, no matter how hot and still the air
might be below. Now she thought of the tree with a new
excitement. For why, if one climbed it at break of day,
could not one see all the world, and easily discover from
whence the white heron flew, and mark the place, and find
the hidden nest?

A. On a separate piece of paper or in your writing notebook, answer each of the following questions. Refer back to the passage to check your answers.

1. Is the pine tree older or younger than other trees in the forest? What details help you answer the question?

2. The author includes details about the words and the things Sylvia knew. For example, Jewett uses the phrases "the stately head" or "great rough trunk." Why are the details important to the passage?

3. Why does Sylvia want to reach the top of the tree? List details that tell you.

4. What mood, or overall feeling, do the details in the passage create?

B. Think about a woods or a park near your home. On a separate piece of paper or in your writing notebook, list details about the place. Is it small or large? What do the trees look like? What else do you see? Write a paragraph about the park or forest, using the details from your list to describe it. Your teacher may want you to share your paragraph with the class.

Writing Activity 4

Read the passage from *Twenty Thousand Leagues Under the Sea* by Jules Verne. In the passage, Captain Nemo, who commands the submarine that will go to the bottom of the sea, identifies instruments.

With a wave of the hand my host indicated the instruments that hung on the walls of his room. "Here," he began, "are the contrivances which control the navigation of the submarine. I have them always under my eyes, and they tell me my position and exact direction in the middle of the ocean. Which ones are known to you?"

"The thermometer, of course, which gives us the internal temperature; and the barometer, which marks the weight of the air and foretells changes in the weather."

"To the left is the hygrometer."

"Which, if its name be any clue, must measure the dryness of the atmosphere. Oh, yes, and next to it is the storm-glass, the contents of which, by decomposing, announce the approach of tempests. And here is the compass which guides your course. But what is the next object?"

A. On a separate piece of paper or in your writing notebook, answer each of the following questions. Refer back to the passage to check your answers.

1. List four instruments mentioned in the passage and tell what they are used for.

2. According to the passage, why does Captain Nemo keep an eye on the instruments?

B. Captain Nemo points out instruments he uses aboard ship. Think about the tools, machines, or instruments you have seen used at home, in school, at a store, in a repair shop, or in some place you have visited. Describe the tools, machines, or instruments and explain their use. How do the types of equipment help identify the place where they are located?

Writing Activity 5

Read the following passage from "Paul Revere's Ride" by
Henry Wadsworth Longfellow.

Listen, my children, and you shall hear
Of the midnight ride of Paul Revere,
On the eighteenth of April, in Seventy-five;
Hardly a man is now alive
Who remembers that famous day and year.

He said to his friend, "If the British march
By land or sea from the town tonight,
Hang a lantern aloft in the belfry arch
Of the North Church tower as a signal light,—
One, if by land, and two, if by sea;
And I on the opposite shore will be,
Ready to ride and spread the alarm
Through every Middlesex village and farm,
For the country folk to be up and to arm."

Then he said, "Good night!" and with muffled oar
Silently rowed to the Charlestown shore,
Just as the moon rose over the bay,
Where swinging wide at her moorings lay
The *Somerset*, British man-of-war;
A phantom ship, with each mast and spar
Across the moon like a prison bar,
And a huge black hulk, that was magnified
By its own reflection in the tide.

A. On a separate piece of paper or in your writing notebook, answer each of the following questions. Refer back to the passage to check your answers.

1. Why was Paul Revere ready to ride? When does Paul Revere ride out? At what time? On what day?

2. What is a belfry arch? What was to be hung in the belfry arch?

3. How would Revere know whether the British were moving by land or by sea? Where does Revere wait for the signal?

4. Check your history book or look up more information to find out what year the ride took place and why it was so famous.

B. Write about the famous ride of Paul Revere. Tell about rowing the boat, getting ready to ride, and the ride. Use details about the people and places. Also use details to tell how Revere might feel, knowing about his responsibility.

Writing Activity 6

Working with another student as your partner, choose a place that you both know, such as a restaurant, a movie theater, or a shopping mall.

List five details about the place. Do not work with your partner while you list the details. The details can give directions, describe the place, or explain why you like the place.

Compare your list with the list made by your partner. Did you each list the same details, or did you choose different details?

Combine the lists and choose six of the details that you like best. Then each of you should write a paragraph using the six details about the place.